The Prestige

Yorkshire Coaching Pools

Keith Healey

© **2003 Keith Healey**

ISBN 1 898432 90 2

Cover: East Yorkshire No. **680** (**6680 KH**), a 1960 Leyland Tiger Cub PSUC1/2 with MCCW dual-purpose 41-seat coachwork, seen in April 1963 at Huntingdon Street bus station, Nottingham, on its way from Hull to Birmingham, was typical of the heavyweight vehicles of that era to be seen on Pool services. *(JBC/GHFA)*

Inside front cover: A Yorkshire Services time- and faretable issued for the period 6th June to 16th September 1957 for Yorkshire - Birmingham - Coventry. *(Courtesy West Yorkshire Information Service)*

Rear cover: Nineteen-thirty-seven summer departures and faretables leaflet for Yorkshire to Blackpool. *(Keith Healey Collection)*

Title page: Leeds bus station in Wellington Street was an interchange point for a variety of routes. Passengers from Blackpool could connect not only to the east coast but also further afield to Newcastle upon Tyne and Middlesbrough. In this August 1949 view vehicles from the East Yorkshire, West Yorkshire, Ribble and Northern General fleets can be seen. *(JBC/GHFA)*

Opposite page: Fred Bibby & Son, of Ingleton, **SKY 46J**, an early 1970s Duple-bodied Bedford was working on hire to West Yorkshire at Bradford and was awaiting its departure time for Blackpool. The Pool relied heavily on hired vehicles to keep services going at summer weekends. *(Keith Healey Collection)*

Below: A busy scene at Nottingham in the 1930s. Coaches have arrived from London and Birmingham and are waiting to carry on northwards to various points in Yorkshire. There was no lack of passengers waiting to board. *(Keith Healey Collection)*

Acknowledgements

From an early age, eight to be exact, I have been intrigued by coach time-tables as well as coaches; buses turned me cold I'm sorry to say. Nearly all my working life was spent in the coaching and travel industry and during the 1950s and 60s I got to know the owners of many coach companies both small and large in the North-West as well as Yorkshire. Sometimes we faced each other across the table at the Traffic Commissioners' hearings; at others we banded together to oppose the big BET or Tilling Companies. Then there was the annual dinner dance, held usually at the Imperial Hotel, Blackpool, where friend and foe could all enjoy themselves.

In this, the third book from Venture Publications on coaching pools, I have to acknowledge once again the writings of Cobbett, Duncan and Michael Jewell in various trade journals over the years; I was reminded by them of licensing decisions whose details I had forgotten even though I was present at some of the hearings.

As always with books in this series, indispensable help has been unstintingly given by a number of people and author and publisher offer grateful thanks to: the Greater Manchester Transport Society for allowing access to their archives; Philip Battersby for information on early services from the North-East; John Gill of the West Yorkshire Information Service, who unravelled many problems; Ron Maybray for information on vehicles from his fleet records; The Omnibus Society and The PSV Circle, whose publications have, as so often, been turned to for the solution to that otherwise unanswerable query; the series editor, John Banks, who has been enthusiastically supportive throughout and has made available many images from his collection *(JBC)*, including the splendid G H F Atkins *(GHFA)* photographs; Mary and David Shaw for reading the proofs and spotting many an elusive gremlin.

Keith Healey,
Altrincham, Cheshire
March 2003

Introduction

To pool resources to operate a service is nothing new in the road passenger transport industry and can be traced back over two hundred years to the time of stage coaches, when for example, the London - Leeds mail coach route comprised eight different contractors to operate the thirty-hour journey between the two centres. The contractors were responsible for providing horses and coachmen in a given area of the route, they had to use special coaches supplied by the body builder under contract to the Government, paying a mileage rental for them. They were allowed to keep the fares and parcel receipts but even in those days evidence was given of "pocketing" the odd fare by the coachman.

The stage and mail coaches were gradually replaced with the commencement of the railways, the coaches then acting as feeders to the railways connecting to towns not reached by the train. Although the country carrier with his bus was gradually coming to the fore in the early part of the twentieth century it was not until after the Great War in 1919 that the internal combustion engine came into its own on long-distance routes.

In 1922 Sidney Garcke, a Director of the British Automobile Traction Company, in a paper to the newly formed Institute of Transport, referred to the boom that had taken place in long distance road travel the previous year due to the various industrial strikes which had affected the railways and their operation. He observed that generally speaking the older established omnibus undertakings had not fallen into the error of participating in the traffic to any serious extent and were therefore not now financially embarrassed by the return to rail of the large proportion of long distance holiday passengers.

By 1926/7 the small independent operator was again looking at the long distance coaching market and had started to develop services throughout Britain. Most of the large bus companies had been formed by either British Electric Traction from former tramway operators, or their subsidiary British Automobile Traction in which Thomas Tilling held shares and lastly Thomas Tilling in their own right. In 1928 the BAT name was changed to Tilling and British Automobile Traction Co Ltd which brought Tilling into partnership with the BET. The following year the mainline railway companies purchased shares in each of the T&BAT companies: this meant that the railways held a similar number of shares in each company as did T&BAT, neither having a controlling interest. At the same time the railways also purchased shares in some companies directly owned by BET. All these companies with railway interest were always referred to as the Associated Companies.

The railways were now concerned with the long distance services operated by the independents and suggested that the Associated Companies should also consider operating express services. Many General Managers felt they were being forced into something of which they had no intimate knowledge. They were also aware of the regulations which the new Transport Minister, Herbert Morrison, would be introducing to Parliament in the near future based on the Royal Commission on Transport Report, and if they did not act quickly they might be left behind when the Act came into force - or did the introduction of the new Leyland TS chassis, which was appearing on the market, help? Whatever the reason, 1929 saw the commencement of long-distance services on both sides of the Pennines by the Associated Companies.

In July 1930, W J Thomson of Scottish Motor Traction gave a paper to the Institute of Transport on long distance travel: that Company by this time was linking Scotland to London by day and night services. However, comments on the paper summed up certain individuals' feelings, none more so than O C Power, Traffic Manager of the Birmingham & Midland Motor Omnibus Company, who claimed he had commenced the first service of over 100 miles in length ten years previously between Birmingham and Weston - super - Mare and at the present time he operated more long distance services than any other operator. He also stated that none of them made a profit if proper costing was done and that the local services sustained the long-distance services, but he was forced to operate them if he was to keep ahead of his competitors. He felt the proposed rigid thirty miles per hour speed limit and the five and a half hour driving time would

be the death of the long-distance routes of 100 miles or more. He would rather have the elastic twenty miles per hour and get caught every now and again. Other operators felt that long-distance travel was the province of the railways and that road operators should provide feeder services to link with the railways; many thought that congestion on the roads would result in passengers returning to the railway. While up to a hundred miles might be acceptable in the summer months, fifty miles was the most in the winter.

It is a miracle that long distance services survived in the face of these views expressed by such prominent figures. Although jointly run services were quite common prior to the commencement of the Road Traffic Act in 1931, it was usually on the basis of each operator keeping his own receipts but with interchangeable return tickets. The first long-distance pool, which involved four different operators, was the Manchester - Leeds - Newcastle upon Tyne service, which commenced in 1929. The format used in the "Limited Stop" Pool was to continue with the Yorkshire company pools, with each operator having a fixed mileage and receipts entitlement after the deductions of Pool expenses: these would include omnibus station charges, legal charges (applications before the Traffic Commissioners, solicitors' charges, appeal decision costs), lodgings for drivers and conductors, trunk telephone calls, publicity, agents' commissions etc., with one company taking on the role of accountant.

After the introduction of Road Service Licensing, Chairmen of the Traffic Commissioners, in various Traffic Areas, were concerned at the high number of express services which were licensed but were competing with each other not only on route but on departure times as well, and gentle hints were made to operators about coordinating services common among them or the Commissioners might have to take action.

Yorkshire Services Pool

The beginning 1928-35

The route from Yorkshire to London was pioneered by the small independent, in fact this

was the case throughout Northern England. One of the first applications for a licence to operate to London was by Mr F G Wood of Burnley who, in 1927, sought one from the Sheffield authorities; there is no evidence that the route operated. The South Yorkshire Motor Services was considered to be the first with a route between Leeds and London in late 1927 using Studebaker coaches. By 1928 further routes were opened with services between Sheffield and London by Underwood Express using Gilfords with 26-seat Strachan and Brown bodies. Coachways were operating between Leeds and London with Dennis E types bodied by Hall Lewis, the 20-seat bodies were described as "high body", enabling luggage to be stored underneath the vehicle in lockers instead of on the roof. Other concerns operating from Leeds were two London independent bus operators, Harris & Matthews, and Heather Motor Services; the latter stated in their adverts that their vehicles had interior heating and lighting and separate armchair seats with writing tables. The service later started from Bradford. Lastly Hale Coachways who, for a short while, ran from Hull also. Bentinck Motors (B&E Services) operated from Bradford, and even the Blackpool

operator W Armitage (Progress Motors), who had opened a garage in Huddersfield, was reported as running from that town to London. If, however, you lived in York or Doncaster you were even better off. All the services from the North-East called at either or both of these two points on their way to and from London. In the period 1928-30 at least 18 different companies were involved on this route.

The West Yorkshire Road Car Company was among the first of the Associated Companies to operate long-distance services. Commencing ex-Yorkshire on Friday 19 July 1929 from Harrogate to London, using the London Coastal coach station at 1a Lupus Street as the southern terminal, connections were provided at Leeds from Bradford, York, Ripon and Scarborough. The recently delivered Roe-bodied Leyland TS2 Tiger 26-seaters were put on the route. On the same day East Yorkshire Motor Services commenced a service to London from Scarborough, also using Leyland TS2s but with Hall Lewis 26-seat coachwork. Both companies operated independently of each other, in many cases competing at various towns en route.

In August West Yorkshire started a second route from Harrogate, this time to Birmingham,

Above: A precursor of activity on the road between London and Kingston upon Hull was this De Dion Bouton, registered **YX 9297** in late 1928. Its proprietors are believed to have been Messrs Johnson & Neale, about whom no details have been traced. The photograph was taken at Grantham on 5th August 1929. *(JBC/GHFA)*

Below: About a year later, and also in Grantham, a Wilks of Leeds 20-seat Gilford **UA 9251** has just disgorged its passengers for a refreshment stop. Wilks later formed part of B&E. *(JBC/GHFA)*

and again East Yorkshire began a service to Birmingham from Scarborough with a connecting service from Hull which served the London route as well.

By now South Yorkshire were operating three times a day to the Capital City: they had opened waiting rooms at Leeds and Doncaster with an attendant in charge. It was stated that night travellers especially would appreciate this accommodation. They had also introduced through bookings to various destinations on the south coast and were looking at the Dennis and Albion chassis for the service.

There were other companies operating to London during the same period apart from those already mentioned. Queen Line Coaches of Willesden operated daily from London to Hull as did Fleetways of Hampole near Doncaster. An experimental sleeper service was introduced by Road Sleeper (Leeds) Ltd to Bradford but this did not last long with the company going into liquidation in late 1929. There was Wilks Parlour Coaches from Leeds: Wilks was a terminal agent with various operators using his garage in Leeds as a picking-up point. He experimented with a London service perhaps taking over one of the failed operators' routes. Another service from Sheffield was operated by Premier Sunshine Saloons; sometimes licensed by Sheffield, it continued running until October 1931 after losing its appeal for a licence under the new Road Traffic Act. Hexby and Tealey of Retford using the fleet name of Ne Plus Ultra Services also operated from Sheffield commencing on either August 1st or 8th 1928 - both dates have been quoted. How long the service lasted is unknown with the company being taken over by the London and North Eastern Railway early in 1929, but there was no mention of a London service by then.

Scarborough also seemed very popular with both Ovington Motors of York and Blue Band Bus Services of Middlesbrough linking the resort to London. Another short lived service was by Gladwyn Parlour Coaches of Mansfield operating from that town via Nottingham. There were plans to extend the service northwards but they tried to expand too quickly and ceased in early December 1928. Their local services around Mansfield became part of the Ebor Bus Company. Their main claim to fame

were the two Reeve and Kenning bodies on W&G chassis which were divided into three compartments with the centre section having a raised observation above the normal roof.

By now two other Associated Companies were considering operating to London. The former tramway companies Yorkshire (WD) Electric Tramways and the Barnsley & District Electric Traction were BET subsidiaries with Barnsley & District changing its name to Yorkshire Traction Co Ltd after its transfer to the T&BAT group. After consultations with West Yorkshire Road Car, jointly operated services among the three were commenced on Thursday, 3rd July 1930 to London. One route ran from Harrogate and the second started from Keighley; by interchanging at Barnsley a full range of picking up points and destinations could be covered. There were also two routes to Birmingham on the same principal. All services were operated under the title "Yorkshire Services", a name that was to be used until the formation of National Travel 43 years later. The new operators also used the Leyland TS chassis, Yorkshire (WD) with Roe 26-seat coachwork and Yorkshire Traction with Brush 26-seaters although they still had some with Hall Lewis bodies delivered in 1929. East Yorkshire, not to be outdone, had named their operation "East Coast Express" for services from Scarborough and "Southern Express" from Hull. In 1931 East Yorkshire joined the other three in joint operation of the Yorkshire services and at the same time West Yorkshire withdrew their feeder service from Scarborough which had operated in opposition to East Yorkshire and other operators.

The last operator to join the Yorkshire Services Pool was East Midland Motor Services in 1934 who operated a service from Sheffield via Chesterfield, Alfreton and Derby to London. Although Derby was served on the Birmingham routes this was the first time the Pool was able to offer it for London. The service was originally started by Underwood Express Services of Sheffield on July 12th 1928 and by October of that year it had expanded into a daily service. W T Underwood, the owner, had been employed by United Automobile who, in 1920, had commenced operation in Derbyshire based at Clowne under the name of W T Underwood. In

Above: In 1933, South Yorkshire and B&E merged their London routes to form London, Midland & Yorkshire Services. B&E's 1932 Beadle-bodied 32-seat Leyland Tiger TS4 No. **16 (DT 3697)** is seen in Nottingham, returning to Bradford, in about 1934. *(JBC/GHFA)*

Below: In another prewar Nottingham view, Yorkshire Woollen District Brush-bodied Leyland Lion LT1 No. **123 (HD 3765)**, a 30-seat service bus, had been brought in at short notice to duplicate the Birmingham service. *(JBC/GHFA)*

1927 Underwood left the Company which was renamed East Midland Motor Services. Underwood then moved to Sheffield and as well as a London service he also operated from that city to Manchester and Blackpool. He also sought to extend the service to London by applying for licences in Leeds and Wakefield which, though granted, were not taken up because on 1st February 1930 the services were taken over jointly by the LMS and LNE Railways and they were granted the transfer of licences by Sheffield. The London service was later passed to the now railway-owned East Midland company. The route to Manchester was combined with the railways' own service and the Blackpool service was, for a time, operated by East Midland on behalf of the railways before being passed to the newly formed Sheffield United Tours in 1935. Later in 1930 East Midland was passed to the T&BAT group, which owned half of the shares with the railways having the other half. East Midland brought a new chassis onto the route: the AEC Regal with a Brush 30-seat body; by 1936 the company had turned to Leyland for coaches.

There were still the independent operators who had received licences from the newly formed Traffic Commissioners and the joint operators were looking at the possibility of purchasing these companies. The first to be purchased, in 1933, was Hale Garage and Coachways who operated between Leeds and London via Newark, Stamford and Papworth. According to correspondence between Yorkshire Traction and the Traffic Commissioners dated 15th June 1933 they had acquired a financial interest in Hales and it would seem to have been operated as a subsidiary for a time. The other operators were B&E Motors from Bradford via Nottingham, Leicester and Northampton - they were also the only company to operate a night service; Wilks Parlour Coaches from Leeds via Newark, Grantham and Stamford; the last was South Yorkshire also from Leeds travelling through Newark, Stamford and Baldock.

B&E had been originally owned by E J Heath and G H Ennifer; the initials stood for Bentick and Ensign: the former because of the street where the head office was; the latter for G H Ennifer of Blue Ensign Motor Services.

Ennifer later withdrew from B&E, but carried on with Blue Ensign. The Wilks company was purchased by B&E, this gave that company an alternative route to London which followed closely the South Yorkshire route. The two companies decided to coordinate their routes under the title of London Midland and Yorkshire Services and were finally purchased by Yorkshire Services in 1935.

The final route to be taken over was the Phillipson's Motor Coaches Ltd service between Scarborough and Doncaster originally operated by Ovington Motors Ltd of York between Scarborough and London via York. In October 1930 Ovington was purchased by United Automobile Services; the purchase included eight vehicles and two local routes. There was a clause that excluded the long-distance services the company and shareholders were interested in. In January 1931 W A Kay, one of Ovington's shareholders, formed London and East Coast Motors Ltd to operate the Scarborough - London service. Another Ovington shareholder, Frank Hersey, was involved with Phillipson's. Hersey was the London end of the business with premises at 8 York Road, Kings Cross. During 1931 Phillipson's, who operated from Sunderland to London, hired from L&EC four AEC Regals to operate the service. At a meeting held in January 1932 it was suggested that Phillipson's purchased the L&EC business subject to the transfer of the Scarborough licences and the assets to include the four coaches. It was not until July 1933 that Kay became a Director of Phillipson's having the same number of shares as had both Hersey and Phillipson. On 7th September 1934 the Company was sold to United Automobile who appointed their own Directors and the Registered Office was transferred from London to Darlington. Yorkshire Services then applied for the Scarborough - Doncaster summer service link which had connected with Phillipson's London service. So ended the competition on the London routes.

Operation of the Pool 1936-9

The main line railways always considered that long-distance road services were there for one reason only - to take business away from the

"YORKSHIRE SERVICES" ROUTES

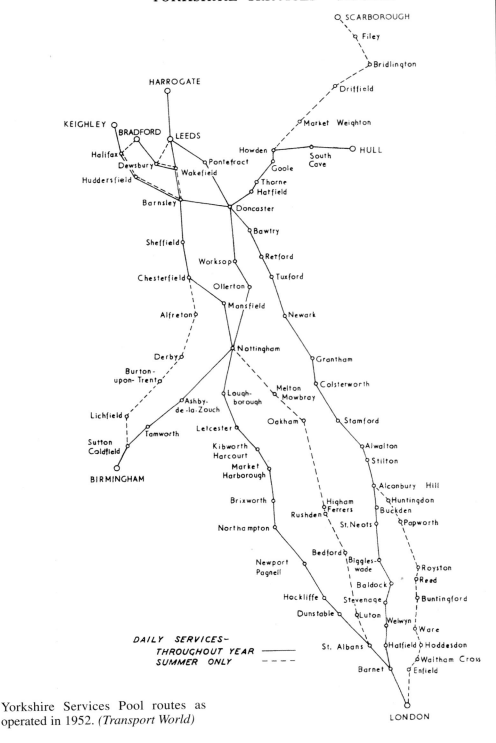

DAILY SERVICES—
THROUGHOUT YEAR ———
SUMMER ONLY - - - -

Yorkshire Services Pool routes as
operated in 1952. (Transport World)

railways: they did not agree, as was true in most cases, that road operators generated new passengers who would not have travelled by rail; they persuaded the Minister in appeal cases that routes that were not of a tourist or holiday nature were abstracting traffic from the railway and that the latter should be protected. This brought about the Road Service Licences (Appeals) Order (No. 54), 1933, which was originally framed because of an appeal by the LMSR against licences granted to five companies operating between Liverpool and London. It was to reduce the duplication allowance: the number of additional vehicle journeys to be operated on any one day and in any one direction should not exceed three times the minimum number of vehicle journeys required each day in that direction throughout the year under the terms of the licences. Although at first it referred to the above route in the North Western Traffic Area, the railways used it to try and reduce duplication on various other routes in other Traffic Areas quoting the Minister's decision. This brought problems to services that were taken over, especially to London, and many companies were kept on as subsidiaries in order to keep the duplication allowance: it was not until a few years later that Traffic Commissioners granted extra duplicates and even then a very strong case had to be made.

In 1936 a formal agreement was reached by the members of the Yorkshire Services Pool on the mileage and revenue entitlement of each company. It came into force as from 1st October 1934 - the date of the inclusion of the East Midland Motor Services Sheffield - London route.

On the Yorkshire - London route the original four operators were entitled to 22% each of the mileage operated while East Midland's entitlement was 12%. The Yorkshire - Birmingham entitlement was 25% to each of the Yorkshire Companies with East Midland not having any entitlement: EMMS was not, in fact, licensed to operate to Birmingham until a few years later. On the Hull - Barnsley feeder service only one third of the mileage was allocated to the Pool, this being split between London and Birmingham mileage.

Clause 13 of the agreement is of interest as it gave East Midland the right to renegotiate its entitlement of the receipts if the car mileage substantially reduced and such reduction was, in the opinion of East Midland, due to variations in the operation of the Yorkshire - Birmingham services. Whereas this would not affect the percentage received by East Midland, it would affect the average rate payable to that company.

There was still competition on the Yorkshire Services Pool routes to Birmingham with the Fawdon Omnibus Company route between Newcastle upon Tyne and Coventry via Leeds and Derby. Having commenced in 1928, they were one of the various concerns linking the North East with the Midlands at that time - these included the Great North of England Omnibus Company service to Nottingham, known as the "Coalfields Express", operated with 24-seat Gilfords; and Diamond Road Coaches of Stanley, who ran to Sheffield; James Kane of Choppington had applied for a service to Leicester but it is not thought to have been operated. Blue Band Bus Services were in August operating a daily service between Newcastle upon Tyne and Birmingham while Underwood Express were applying for licences to operate between Newcastle upon Tyne and Chesterfield. Another service, begun in 1930 by Hall Bros, of South Shields, was from Newcastle upon Tyne to Nottingham later extended to Leicester then Coventry. Only Fawdon and Hall Bros obtained licences in 1931 under the new Road Traffic Act. The Fawdon service ran parallel with the Newcastle upon Tyne - Leeds service operated by the Limited Stop Pool. In 1933 Fawdon was purchased by West Yorkshire on behalf of the two Pools. Hall Bros remained independent until taken over by Barton Transport in July 1967 who then operated until the route was merged with National Express. When the Fawdon service was taken over the idea had been to operate in the summer only with the winter traffic being catered for by changing at Leeds. After taking into account the Hall Bros service which, while not duplicating the route, could be regarded as a competitor, the service was operated throughout the year.

There was a separate agreement for the Fawdon service with the route mileage being split at Leeds for mileage and receipts

Above: Taken in August 1929, a few days after the inauguration of the service to Birmingham, is West Yorkshire No. **502** (**WW 9049**), a recently delivered Leyland Tiger TS2 fitted with Roe 26-seat coachwork. The headboard carries the words "Limited Stop": "Yorkshire Services" was substituted in 1930. *(JBC/GHFA)*

Below: AEC Regal No. **LC20** (**VO 5620**) of East Midland Motor Services is seen in as-built condition, before delivery into the EMMS fleet. The 30-seat coachwork was by Brush. It carries route boards for the ex-Underwood service used before the merger with Yorkshire Services in 1934. *(JBC)*

entitlements. The 94 miles northwards from Leeds was shared by Yorkshire (WD), West Yorkshire, Northern General and North Western Road Car each being allocated 25%; these were all members of the Limited Stop Pool. The route south of Leeds, 123 miles, was allocated to the Yorkshire Services Pool members, West Yorkshire, Yorkshire (WD), Yorkshire Traction and East Yorkshire each again having 25% of the mileage. The receipts were accordingly divided in the same way: for example, the fare between Newcastle and Coventry was 216 old pence, this being allocated 94/216ths to the Limited Stop Pool and 123/216ths to the Yorkshire Services Pool. The licence was held in the name of Fawdon Omnibus Company of Bensham - the Head Office of Northern General who acted as accountants. Because Fawdon no longer owned any vehicles a hiring permit was granted by the Traffic Commissioners with the service first operated by Northern General; later West Yorkshire and Yorkshire (WD), who had the largest mileage entitlement, took over the operation. Although the other companies took part in duplication on this service there was one exception, North Western Road Car, who ran off their share of the mileage on the Limited Stop Pool instead. The outbreak of the Second World War saw the termination of the routes for the duration.

In 1939 the services operated by the Yorkshire Services Pool were:

A   Harrogate - London via Great North Road
B   Bradford - London via Sheffield, Nottingham and Bedford
C   Leeds - Birmingham via Doncaster and Nottingham
D   Keighley - Birmingham via Barnsley and Derby
E   Bridlington - Birmingham via Scarborough, Leeds and Derby
F   Scarborough - London via Bridlington, Doncaster and Northampton
G   Bradford - London via Great North Road and Royston
H   Halifax - London via Derby and Bedford
I   Barnsley - London via Sheffield, Nottingham and Bedford
J   Bradford - London via Leeds, Sheffield and Nottingham
K   Hull - Barnsley via Selby
L   Newcastle upon Tyne - Coventry via Leeds and Birmingham
M   Bradford - London via Sheffield, Nottingham and Northampton

Service M ran in the winter period only and services B E F G H I and J operated in the summer period only with service J being an overnight service and all the others operating daily throughout the year. During the summer A B D and K interchanged at Barnsley and A C and F also interchanged at Doncaster so that passengers had a choice of two routes to Birmingham and three to London. Services B C and F also converged again at Nottingham. Services E and L were timed to arrive in Barnsley at 1.45pm in time to connect with service I giving passengers from the east coast facilities to Coventry and London. Services G and H operated independently but offered an earlier arrival in London so that connections to the south coast could be made.

Recommencement 1946-73

Although a permit was granted in 1946 to recommence the London and Birmingham services there seems to be some doubt as to when the services actually started: the earliest time table is dated 18th July 1947. It was a very restricted service with not all the prewar services, including the overnight service, reinstated.

In 1951, some four years later, application was made for the restoration of the night service plus improved use of duplication. The night service was granted but only for the summer months although this now commenced in May instead of July as in 1939. The Easter and Christmas operation was refused together with the amended duplication. In 1952 a further application was made to reintroduce services which had not operated after the war including two routes, one via Stamford and Royston and the other via Nottingham and Bedford. At the same time application was made to bring the duplication allowance back to that granted in 1939. The present allowance was three service

Above: A 1932 Leyland Tiger TS2, No. **363** (**HE 5640**), with Weymann 32-seat coachwork, from the Yorkshire Traction fleet seen in Nottingham on the Bradford to London service. As did West Yorkshire at that time, Yorkshire Traction used preprinted destination boards instead of roller blinds. *(JBC/GHFA)*

Below: East Midland AEC Regal No. **LC18** (**VO 5618**), fitted with 32-seat coachwork by Brush, is seen in the mid-1930s participating in its owner's share of the Yorkshire to London pool. The enlarged destination screen (compare with VO 5620 on page 13) is evident. *(JBC/GHFA)*

cars plus five duplicate journeys a day in each direction. The application was to have five service cars plus eight duplicates while an extra five duplicates could be operated on Saturdays from the last Saturday in July to the first Saturday in September inclusive, these to be used for passengers travelling between London and Scarborough, Bridlington or Harrogate. It was desired that, instead of having a duplication allowance to each route, all routes should be classed together with the overall duplication allowance covering all routes so that full advantage could be taken to carry traffic instead of fixing restrictions on certain services: this would help the night service, which under the present system had no duplicate allowance. A schedule was drawn up showing that during the period July to September 1951, a total of 92 days, on 75 of those days the full allowance was used whilst on the other 17 days, which were mid week, there was only one vehicle less than the maximum allowance. From June 1951, after the refusal of the duplication allowances, names and addresses were taken and a total of 1,346 passengers had been refused in that period. It does seem that it was March 1954 before the duplication problem was solved and it was agreed that an overall allowance covering all routes should be made. During the winter period it was defined as two service cars with six additional vehicles to be operated in any one direction on any one day; during Easter and Christmas period the allowance was increased to eight. During the summer period, defined as the Thursday before Whit Sunday to the third Sunday in September, five service cars were operated with eight additional journeys plus a further five from the end of July to the beginning of September on Saturdays only to Harrogate, Scarborough, Bridlington and Filey. So after a long struggle the London services returned to more or less their prewar running but with a more viable operation possible.

Evidence had been given of a link between Yorkshire Services and Thos Cook & Son Ltd whereby the latter offered inclusive holidays in Harrogate including hotel accommodation and excursions while Yorkshire Services offered through Thos Cook inclusive holidays from Yorkshire to London and in 1951 2,250 passengers had enjoyed the facilities.

In late 1954 an application was made to delete Papworth and substitute Cambridge, and further application was made to introduce, on Saturdays only, a 5.25am Doncaster - Scarborough journey returning from Scarborough at 7.45pm. This was to connect with the overnight service to/from London.

In 1955 there was a railway strike and duplication restrictions were lifted by the Traffic Commissioners on express services in order to meet the expected public demand. However, the North East of England was a National Union of Railwaymen stronghold and train services were almost normal and the traffic carried by Yorkshire Services was only 25% above the same period the previous year.

The following year Yorkshire Services made application to operate an extra two duplicates on their London Service. This brought about a strong objection from the railways who rather spoilt their case by saying there was no evidence of extra traffic being carried by Yorkshire Services and the duplication allowance should revert back to the 1935 figure. Needless to say the Traffic Commissioners did not agree with the statement and granted the extra duplicates. Evidence was given that there had been a great increase in bookings onto the Continent by the coach/air services offered from London.

Appearing before the Traffic Commissioners either objecting to or applying for licences could at times provide a bit of light relief as the author knows from his appearances in the various Traffic Areas. For example, if Lancashire were playing at home you could guarantee any hearing in Manchester would finish early due to a certain Chairman being a cricket fan. Another Chairman had a habit of looking as though he had nodded off, especially during cross-examination, then throwing in a question that caught everyone unawares. Such was an application by an independent operator to run an excursion to dog shows throughout the country in 1956, which caused Yorkshire Services to object as the application included towns served by them. The service was to be only for dog breeders, exhibitors and their dogs, which rather took Yorkshire Services aback. The boot of the coach was ventilated for small dogs and larger animals travelled inside. Yorkshire Services quickly accepted a

Above: A small number of Daimlers with 28-seat coachwork by Brush was purchased by Yorkshire Traction in 1933. One of them, No. **369** (**HE 5992**), is seen in Nottingham operating as a duplicate from Birmingham to Barnsley. *(JBC/GHFA)*

Below: Once East Yorkshire had joined the Pool in 1932, its Scarborough service became host to the vehicles of the other participants. Here, in another 1930s Nottingham picture, Yorkshire Traction No. **429** (**HE 6342**), a 1934 Leyland Tiger TS6 with Eastern Counties 28-seat coachwork, is seen *en route* for the resort. *(JBC/GHFA)*

restriction to one vehicle and withdrew their objection. Major F S Eastwood, Chairman of the Yorkshire Commissioners observed: "I don't suppose the Yorkshire Pool want a couple of mastiffs on the back seat".

Yorkshire Services were looking at ways of increasing traffic and by 1957 through services were being operated via London to the south coast with vehicles going on hire to Maidstone & District to Hastings and Bexhill and Southdown Motor Services to Brighton and Eastbourne for journeys south of London.

In 1958 changes were being made to the services with the direct London - Scarborough route being replaced with a connection at Leeds onto the West Yorkshire service but during the summer months a Friday night service from London returning Saturday night was operated direct to the resort.

The new motorways encouraged the application in 1962 for a direct Barnsley - London service via the M1.

In August of that year the Fawdon Omnibus Company was wound up with a new licence being held by each company involved in the operation of either the Limited Stop or Yorkshire Services Pools. This meant for the first time Lancashire United Transport held a joint licence as did United Automobile Services and East Midland. The revenue and mileage entitlement was discontinued with each operator being entitled to a fixed mileage if they ran on the service. The new jointly licensed route was to be marketed under the name of "The Ten Cities Express".

In 1965 the service to London via Nottingham and Northampton was terminated at Northampton. With the development of the United Counties routes from that area to London it made the Yorkshire Services route beyond Northampton unnecessary. The following year further through running across London was introduced, this time in conjunction with East Kent Road Car Company to Margate and Ramsgate and this developed into a joint service the following year. In the same year, 1967, the Northampton service was extended to Luton. There were further joint services introduced in 1968 with Southdown Motor Services between Yorkshire and Worthing/Brighton (X82) and Eastbourne (X83).

As more use was made of the motorways a further revision was made on the London service via Cambridge which was terminated at that city providing a once-daily service to Yorkshire with connections available to and from many points in East Anglia in conjunction with Premier Travel and Eastern Counties as well as to Scotland in the reverse direction.

Nineteen-seventy saw the withdrawal of Yorkshire (WD) from the Yorkshire Services Pool when all their coaches were transferred to Hebble Motor Services. The licences were also taken over and Hebble now appeared as a joint operator on the London, Birmingham and Newcastle upon Tyne routes. A new service was introduced from the East Midlands and South Yorkshire direct to Edinburgh and Glasgow in the same year but seems to have disappeared for the 1973 season, being replaced with a service from Sheffield which had been one of the picking up points. The last two joint routes were also introduced. 1971 saw Hastings and Bexhill with Maidstone and District and Portsmouth and Southsea with Southdown the following year.

The thorn in the side of the Associated operators in Yorkshire was Wallace Arnold who fought numerous battles with not only the operators but the Traffic Commissioners as well. In 1972 they hit the jackpot by successfully applying for two services to London: one from York via Leeds and Wakefield; the second commencing from Huddersfield via Bradford, Leeds and Wakefield. They were to be operated only for students between the ages of 18 and 25, restricted to term-time operating out on Friday and returning Sunday; return fares only were available. The main selling point was the fare at only £1.50p compared with £2.95p on Yorkshire Services. There was, of course, an appeal lodged by the London Service operators, Yorkshire Services and United Automobile. One argument was that students would become a privileged class at the expense of other members of the public and schedules were produced showing a potential loss of students on Friday services operated by Yorkshire Services which amounted to revenue of £2,500 a year. The Appeal was dismissed by the Minister who considered the special needs of the student traffic would be met by this service

Above: Yorkshire Woollen District Leyland Lion LT5A No. **290** (**HD 5207**) dated from 1934 and was fitted with Roe 32-seat service-bus bodywork - not such comfortable transport for passengers to Birmingham, on which service the Lion was acting as a duplicate. *(JBC/GHFA)*

Below: In a late 1930s Nottingham scene, three Scarborough to London Leyland Tigers have pulled in for a refreshment stop. East Midland's **B13** (**BAL 613**) was duplicating East Yorkshire No. **308** (**CKH 236**), a 1937 ECW-bodied 28-seater and No. **346** (**DKH 454**), a 1938 Roe-bodied vehicle of the same seating capacity. *(JBC/GHFA)*

and a substantially lower fare was not necessarily inconsistent with the requirements of the Road Traffic Act. Not content with running student coaches from Yorkshire to London Wallace Arnold used its associate company, Evan Evans Tours of London, to apply for similar services from the Capital to various points in England including Yorkshire.

October 1973 saw all express services operated by the National Bus Company subsidiaries come under the control of National Travel (NBC) Ltd - the renamed London Coastal Coaches Ltd. Five area National Travel organisations were set up and in 1974 Hebble Motor Services became one of these companies and was renamed National Travel (North East) Ltd. So after 43 years the pooled services came to an end.

Yorkshire - Blackpool Pool

The Yorkshire - Blackpool picture, as it became known, was the result of many consultations between the Chairmen of the Yorkshire and North Western Traffic Areas to try and cut the number of services operating to the resort from Yorkshire especially in the winter period. To understand the picture fully a brief description of the routes and operators is necessary.

The principal operators from Yorkshire consisted of the West Yorkshire Road Car Company of Harrogate, who had operated a service between Bradford and Blackpool since 16th July 1928, which had been extended to Leeds the following year. By 1932 they were operating jointly with Ribble Motor Services who had commenced in 1930 between Blackpool and Leeds. At first Ribble used the Robert Barr/Wallace Arnold premises at The Calls as their terminus in Leeds, transferring to the West Yorkshire Station in Wellington Street when the service became a joint operation. The service, numbered 37EX in the Ribble series, carried local passengers as well and between Burnley and Blackpool it operated in conjunction with the Ribble independent service 13EX. There was also a joint service in the summer from Leeds via Skipton and Clitheroe, this was numbered 53EX.

Yorkshire (WD) Electric Tramways began operating period returns in the late 1920s from Dewsbury and by 1932 the service had been extended to Ossett travelling via Heckmondwike, Cleckheaton and Brighouse. It was popular: for example, on Saturday, 2nd September 1933 no fewer than 22 duplicate vehicles were operated to Blackpool. The service, together with their route to Scarborough, was unique in that every passenger had a numbered seat on a numbered vehicle. The company stated that they could load and despatch thirty to forty vehicles in five minutes under this system.

Hebble Motor Services, of Halifax, had been operating period returns to Blackpool since the early 1920s. In May 1928 this developed into a daily summer service from Halifax and Hebden Bridge. It was operating throughout the year by the following year and later extended to commence from Bradford. Norman Dean, then General Manager of Yorkshire Traction, recalls in a paper presented to the Omnibus Society in 1959 the fare cutting that took place prior to the introduction of the Road Traffic Act in 1931 when he was Manager of O & C Holdsworth, later to become Hebble Motor Services. The day return fare between Halifax and Blackpool was 7/6d but price cutting by competitors brought it down to 4/0d. He considered it was time something was done about it and advertised a Sunday excursion at 2/6d and booked hundreds of passengers within hours. Unfortunately the Company was fully owned by the railways who instructed him to cancel the excursion as only they were entitled to offer low fares. The excursion did run but the fare slashing served its purpose and there was no more undercutting by the competitors.

Yorkshire Traction, the renamed Barnsley & District, like the other two companies had operated period returns, in their case on Sundays and Bank Holidays. In 1929 they were expanded into a summer daily service from Doncaster and Barnsley.

Apart from the Ribble service there were three other operators from the resort providing services into Yorkshire. Commencing with period return excursions to Huddersfield in 1922 Walker Taylor & Sons, known as Pride of the Road, had by 1928 extended into three daily services to Leeds. William Armitage followed in 1924 again on the period return excursion fares in this case to Leeds and by 1928 had

Above: As we have already seen, traffic was often heavy enough for vehicles less suitable than the front-line coaches to be brought in as duplicates. Yorkshire Woollen's Leyland Tiger TS7 No. **400** (**HD 6316**) was a Roe-bodied 32-seat service bus working to London. *(JBC/GHFA)*

Below: Yorkshire Woollen's No. **633** (**HD 7991**), a 1948 Duple-bodied Leyland Tiger PS1 32-seater, is seen at Derby working the Fawdon service between Newcastle upon Tyne and Coventry. *(JBC/GHFA)*

purchased property in Huddersfield so it could operate early morning departures from Yorkshire to Blackpool. Trading as Progress Motor Coaches they also ran three times daily to Leeds with one timing to and from Barnsley. The last operator was Wood Bros (Blackpool) Ltd: calling themselves John Bull Coaches they had commenced only in September 1928 with twice daily to Leeds and in 1933 one timing ran to and from Fleetwood - the only company to do so. All three of the Blackpool operators increased their services during Yorkshire local wakes periods and also at Blackpool Illuminations with extra timings. This was to try and stagger the vehicles rather than having a lot of duplication on one timing.

To be added to the picture was a daily service operated by R Barr (Leeds) Ltd, at that time incorporating Wallace Arnold Tours, from Leeds to Blackpool. J Bullock & Son, known as B & S Motor Services, ran from Wakefield, B & B Tours from Bradford and Hanson Motor Services from Huddersfield. Lastly, there was the joint service of W Pyne and Son and Seanor & Co. from Harrogate to the resort. There were also many local operators who were licensed to operate from various areas of Yorkshire at that town's holiday periods, their licences were restricted by the Traffic Commissioners after they had a pruning exercise on which the Chairman is quoted as saying: "We achieved a marked measure of progress on at least restoring order out of chaotic conditions prevailing when we took up Office".

This was the position facing the Traffic Commissioners in 1932; there was also a declining market in coach travel during this period, so suggestions were made by both Yorkshire and North Western Traffic Commissioners for the operators to consider a coordination scheme.

The first scheme was proposed by the three Blackpool operators in November 1932 and was granted by the Traffic Commissioners. This was based on each operator withdrawing certain timings that duplicated each other, but in order to preserve their individual identity all three picking up points in Blackpool were used as well as the two terminal points in Leeds. The Bullock service from Wakefield was also included in the scheme which gave two return journeys a day for Wakefield.

The situation was going to change. W C Standerwick, a Blackpool excursion operator, who also operated services to Birmingham and London from the resort, had sold their business to Ribble and North Western in 1932. Wood Bros also operated services to London as well as into Yorkshire and was the second company to sell. This brought pressure on Armitage and Walker Taylor who after a lot of thought decided to also sell to Ribble. By midsummer 1933 all the Blackpool - Yorkshire services were controlled by Ribble. This brought about consultation with the Yorkshire operators and revised plans for joint operation by the eight operators were submitted to the Traffic Commissioners in October 1933. This application meant a new range of services, some licences were for renewal with modifications. Yorkshire Traction's Doncaster - Blackpool service was to be extended to Talbot Road bus station in Blackpool and to operate a winter feeder between Barnsley and Halifax to connect with a service to Blackpool. While Yorkshire (WD) also wished to extend the route in Blackpool plus commencing from Wakefield, Hebble wished to commence from Leeds. Ribble and West Yorkshire, apart from revising the timetable to introduce an extension to Fleetwood, applied for through bookings from various towns in West Yorkshire on stage carriage routes to connect at suitable points on the services.

In an attempt to make all the licences the same instead of some originating in Blackpool and others in Yorkshire, new licences were applied for originating in Yorkshire for the Blackpool operators. All the routes were to be operated jointly by Hebble Motor Services, West Yorkshire Road Car, Yorkshire Traction, Yorkshire (WD), Ribble Motor Services, W Armitage, Walker Taylor and Wood Bros, with the existing licences held by the last three companies to be surrendered if the application for joint operation was granted.

At the hearing objections were received from the LMSR, R Barr (Leeds) Ltd, Wright Bros (Burnley) Ltd and two solicitors acting on behalf of various operators not named. The application was refused by the Traffic Commissioners whose decision was upheld by the Minister in 1934 after hearing an appeal by the applicants. Wright Bros (Burnley) operated

Above: The delivery, in 1949 as the immediate postwar austerity period began to ease, of new vehicles allowed West Yorkshire to replace some of their prewar coaches. **GWX 137**, fleet number **252**, was a Bristol L5G, which would have been a little slow on express work, but which - with its 31 "dual-purpose" seats within the standard ECW service-bus shell - provided more than adequate comfort for passengers on the London service. It was at Grantham in September 1949. *(JBC/GHFA)*

Below: Yorkshire Traction's No. **812** (**BHE 741**), on the other hand, was uncompromisingly to service-bus specification. A Brush-bodied 32-seat Leyland Tiger PS1, it was also new in 1949 and was working on the Birmingham run. *(JBC/GHFA)*

services between East Lancashire and Blackpool and the company was purchased in January 1934 by Ribble thus bringing these services under their control.

On 16th January 1935 at a meeting held in Harrogate and attended by representatives from West Yorkshire, Ribble, Yorkshire (WD), Yorkshire Traction, Hebble and Mr J O Mann on behalf of the three Blackpool companies, a Pooling agreement of the services involved was concluded. Backdated to 1st December 1934, this brought about a proportional revenue entitlement and mileage operated for the five companies concerned as follows:

Operator	%
Ribble Motor Services Ltd	30
West Yorkshire Road Car Co. Ltd	27
Yorkshire Traction Co. Ltd	23
Yorkshire (WD) Elec. Tramways	11
Hebble Motor Services Ltd	9

This was on the understanding the three Blackpool operators' licences would be transferred on the following lines:

Walker Taylor CW129/1 (Blackpool - Leeds) to Yorkshire (WD)

Armitage CA3/1 (Blackpool - Barnsley) to Yorkshire Traction

Armitage CA3/2 (Blackpool - Leeds) to Ribble

Wood Bros CW9/3 (Fleetwood - Leeds) to Yorkshire Traction

However, the takeover applications were to be deferred because a new joint application had been submitted to the Traffic Commissioners, after the appeal decision had been received, who had indicated an early decision and the companies did not want to cause confusion or more objections by adding something new to the application.

It was agreed that the three Blackpool operators would not participate in the running of the present services but they would be kept alive with their timings being operated by the five companies on an "on hire" basis, the final operating day of the three to be January 31st 1935.

February 1st 1935 saw a new timetable booklet issued headed "Express and Limited

Stop Services between Yorkshire and Blackpool (also Fleetwood)" listing the names of the eight operators. Each route had been given a number but not with the prefix "X" - instead they had the prefix "J".

The schedule at that time needed eight vehicles to operate it: two each from Ribble, West Yorkshire and Yorkshire Traction and one each from Yorkshire (WD) and Hebble. Both Yorkshire Traction and Yorkshire (WD) were to operate "on hire" to the Blackpool companies as per the agreement as neither had licences to operate in the winter period. Yorkshire Traction was also involved in sleep-outs in Lancashire to cover their two routes. It is thought that ex-Walker Taylor and Armitage drivers may have been used to save on costs as four vehicles had been transferred from these companies to Yorkshire Traction in the same month. The Huddersfield - Blackpool service that Hebble operated was in conjunction with the Hanson service during the winter months with Hebble operating two weeks out of three.

By the time the full summer timetable came into force on 7th June the application lodged with the Traffic Commissioners had still not been decided so the five operators could not make the savings they had wished. The application made in January was framed differently from the first one that had been lodged. Each route was to be licensed to the eight operators but only one licence would be issued to cover all the operators for each route. The operators were also listed under one address which was East Parade, Harrogate, the Head Office of West Yorkshire Road Car; previously each operator had applied separately stating that it would operate jointly with the other applicants. If this application was granted all the present licences held would be surrendered. After the hearing, at which the decision was reserved, the two Traffic Areas got together and published in July their own scheme which took twenty three pages in Notices and Proceedings and invited objections or representations at a hearing to be held at the end of July. After consultations with the operators, in which it was agreed that the application should be in the names of the five operators and not include the former Blackpool companies which, in fact, was what the operators desired and coordination would take

Above: Another instance of passengers on the Birmingham route being treated to the more Spartan conditions of a basic service bus is provided by Yorkshire Traction Dennis Lancet No. **859** (**CHE 351**), a 1950 vehicle fitted with Brush 32-seat bodywork. *(JBC/GHFA)*

Below: As the fifties took over from the forties the underfloor-engined single-decker - examples of which had been operational before the war - began to appear in quantity. This Yorkshire Woollen District example, **HD 9153**, fleet number **745**, seen heading for Dewsbury, was a 1951 Leyland Royal Tiger with Windover 39-seat coachwork. *(JBC/GHFA)*

place during the winter period with other Yorkshire independent operators, the two Traffic Areas made a grant which enabled the Pool to operate their new timetable from 1st November 1935 and all the licences held by the eight operators were surrendered. Neither of the Traffic Areas had liked the idea of one licence covering a multitude of operators though the Yorkshire Area when making the grant did go as far as giving the five members who formed the Pool a special reference number BY15 but still issued a separate licence to each operator under that reference number. The North Western Area continued with their usual system with each operator having a separate licence granted to them for each route which followed on from the last licence number issued in their area to that particular Company.

The new services all converged on Burnley from towns in Yorkshire over various routes then to Preston, Lytham St Annes and Blackpool, terminating at Talbot Road bus station with one journey a day extended to Fleetwood. The winter coordination by the Traffic Commissioners was that the service from Huddersfield at 9.00am to Blackpool returning at 3.00pm should now be operated jointly with J Bullock as well as Hanson, operating on a three-week cycle. The timings seemed to discourage day return traffic to the resort but both Bullock and Hanson return tickets were available on the Pool service departing Blackpool at 6.45pm changing at Burnley to the 9.00pm feeder to Halifax and Huddersfield. As the Bullock service originated at Wakefield they were authorised on the weeks they were not operating to run a feeder coach from Wakefield to and from Huddersfield to connect.

During the summer months there was an additional route from Leeds via Skipton, Clitheroe and Whalley to Preston and Blackpool. West Yorkshire provided a connection between Harrogate and Skipton thus competing with the Pyne and Seanor joint service from Harrogate.

During 1934 and 1935 the Yorkshire companies had been consolidating their position by purchasing small independent operators who in some cases operated a service to Blackpool. Yorkshire Traction had taken

over in March 1934 Albert Bentley of Smithies, Barnsley, and on 17th November Lancashire and Yorkshire Motors of Doncaster was purchased with services to Blackpool from Doncaster, Goldthorpe and Upton. Ten days later E Mills (Barnsley) Ltd with a service from High Green and Barnsley to Blackpool was taken over. West Yorkshire Road Car had also purchased the Leeds excursion operator A E Keeling with a Blackpool service via Pudsey.

All these services were a summer operation and only return fares to Blackpool were available. Although they were shown in the Yorkshire - Blackpool timetable leaflet, even allocated a "J" route number, they were not included in the five-operator Pool but, instead, to the general Yorkshire - Blackpool Pool with the routes being operated and licensed to the company who had made the original purchase.

Yorkshire Traction took over the Wilson Haigh excursion and express licences from the Huddersfield Joint Omnibus Committee after HJOC had purchased that company, retaining the stage carriage routes. Although there was a Holmfirth - Blackpool service with a joining point at Huddersfield the service never appeared in the Pool timetable leaflet. When making the grant the Traffic Commissioners had looked at various other independent Yorkshire operators and reconfirmed the condition made in 1932 that during the winter months and between Easter and Whitsuntide the W Pyne and Seanor joint Harrogate - Blackpool route should be operated in conjunction with the Leeds - Blackpool service operated by R Barr (Leeds) Ltd, later Wallace Arnold, and the B & B Tours Bradford - Blackpool route. The route from Leeds interchanged at Otley and passengers on the Bradford route were interchanged at Whalley. To further complicate the matter from the Thursday following Easter to the Wednesday preceding Whitsuntide the interchange of passengers from Leeds was at Gisburn instead of Otley. There would be a four-week cycle with Pyne and Seanor operating a feeder from Harrogate to connect with the other operators on the weeks they did not run.

In 1936 Yorkshire (WD) took over the excursion licences of E Box and Son, of Dewsbury, who had a service to Blackpool. Yorkshire (WD) then applied for a Dewsbury -

Above: Passengers in the early years of underfloor-engined stock were still liable to be faced with service-buses as operators found themselves with insufficient coaches to meet demand. In this view, No. **921** (**DHE 352**), a 1951 Brush-bodied 43-seat Leyland Royal Tiger from the Yorkshire Traction fleet, is seen at Derby operating as far as Birmingham on the Fawdon Newcastle to Coventry service. *(JBC/GHFA)*

Below: More luxurious conditions for London passengers were provided by East Midland's No. **C23** (**PVO 623**), a 1954 Leyland Tiger Cub fitted with Burlingham Seagull coachwork. *(JBC/GHFA)*

Blackpool service via Batley, Birstall and Birkenshaw operating on summer Saturdays only and surrendering the Box licence. Again although given a "J" number it remained licensed to and operated by Yorkshire (WD).

The following year West Yorkshire Road Car purchased the business of Seanor and Company of Harrogate, which meant that their portion of the Harrogate - Blackpool service passed to that company, which became joint operators with W Pyne. Once more a "J" number was allocated but the service remained licensed to and operated by West Yorkshire and the winter coordination continued now with Wallace Arnold and B & B Tours.

One anomaly that remained on the faretable right until the end was that day return tickets were available only from Yorkshire to Blackpool and not vice-versa. Passengers from Blackpool were expected to pay the three month return fare. However, the day return fare from Yorkshire could be extended by contacting the Blackpool offices and paying the appropriate surcharge if you wanted to stay over in the resort.

In order to encourage traffic there was ticket interavailability with other routes: all the East Lancashire - Blackpool services over common points; from Skipton on the United Automobile Middlesbrough service; and between Preston and Blackpool with North Western Road Car and Lancashire United Transport on the X60/X70 from Manchester.

During the Blackpool Illuminations special late journeys were operated back to Yorkshire and half-day return fares were available enabling passengers to leave Yorkshire just after lunch to see the lights.

By 1938 the Yorkshire - Blackpool services had settled into a regular pattern with an attractive leaflet for the services being printed in colour with a bathing beauty and Blackpool Tower on the front. After the outbreak of the Second World War in September 1939 the Pool services continued with a reduced service through 1940 and 1941 but had to be terminated in common with other services by 1942.

By 1939 the following services were operated by the Yorkshire - Blackpool Pool:

J1 Leeds - Fleetwood via Bradford, Colne and Accrington
J2 Leeds - Blackpool via Bradford, Colne and Padiham
J3 Leeds - Blackpool via Bradford, Halifax and Hebden Bridge
J4 Leeds - Blackpool via Bradford, Shelf, Halifax and Hebden Bridge
J5 Leeds - Blackpool via Pudsey and Skipton
J6 Bradford - Skipton feeder service
J7 Doncaster - Blackpool via Barnsley, Huddersfield and Halifax
J8 Wakefield - Blackpool via Dewsbury, Halifax and Hebden Bridge
J9 Leeds - Blackpool via Otley and Skipton
J10 Leeds - Blackpool via Huddersfield and Halifax
J11 High Green - Blackpool via Barnsley
J12 Barnsley - Halifax feeder service
J13 Huddersfield - Burnley feeder service
J14 Huddersfield - Blackpool via Halifax and Hebden Bridge
J15 Dewsbury - Blackpool via Bradford, Skipton and Clitheroe
J16 Harrogate - Blackpool (Joint with W Pyne)

Services 1, 2, 8, 12, 13, 14 and 16 operated throughout the year; the others in the summer period only. Service 6 provided connections with service 9, service 12 with service 8 and service 13 with service 1.

A new start 1946-60

The services recommenced in 1946 more or less operating as before the war but fares had to be increased because of increased costs of fuel, wages, etc. The normal increase was 16 2/3% but the day returns from Yorkshire were increased by 25%.

In September 1950 J Bullock & Sons, known as B & S Motor Services, was acquired by the West Riding Automobile Company. This meant that the Bullock entitlement during the winter months was now taken over by West Riding with their vehicles operating on a Pool route for the first time. The following summer saw the Dewsbury - Blackpool service operated by Yorkshire Woollen District reappear in the

Above: Sometimes operators made a policy of using service buses on express work: in the case of Yorkshire Traction, new vehicles were painted in a reversed livery more appropriate to coaching duties, but they were still service buses. Number **1022** (**GHE 22**), a Tiger Cub with SARO 44-seat bodywork, seen at Nottingham heading from Birmingham to Leeds, was typical of this type of vehicle. After a season or two, they would be repainted in service-bus livery. *(JBC/GHFA)*

Below: Also on its way from Birmingham, in this case going to Doncaster, Yorkshire Traction's **HHE 181**, fleet number **1030**, was a rather more suitable Willowbrook-bodied dual-purpose 39-seat Leyland Tiger Cub. *(JBC/GHFA)*

timetable although it had been operated in previous years.

In 1952 B & B Tours, of Bradford, owned since 1935 by Samuel Ledgard, became after the death of the latter a new Company called Samuel Ledgard (Bradford) Ltd. They operated as per the agreement in the winter months with the Pool and Wallace Arnold. In October 1954 Ledgard applied to withdraw from the coordinated service, which was granted by the Traffic Commissioners. Although they were shown as joint operators in the 1954/5 winter timetable it is unlikely that they participated. This was also the first time since the services recommenced in 1946 that mention was made that some routes were operated jointly with other operators in the winter.

On the Fylde Coast there had been during the Second World War numerous RAF Camps and, at the end of the war, leave coaches were arranged by the camp authorities to various points in England. The licensing authorities were not happy with the private hire principal of operation and felt that they should be operated under road service licences, possibly as period excursions. Ribble already had licences from Warton RAF Camp to destinations including Leeds. In 1954 the Pool applied to introduce special journeys from Weeton RAF Camp to be operated in accordance with the requirements of the camp. Later in the year these journeys were transferred to the Ribble Warton RAF Camp licence enabling both camps to be served by Ribble.

Coach/air facilities

In order to increase traffic an area being looked at was the coach/air facility enabling through bookings to be made. Many claims for the first genuine service have appeared over the years mainly from the East Kent Road Car Company to the Continent or Royal Blue and Southdown to the Isle of Wight. In the case of the North-West the first service was via Blackpool to the Isle of Man introduced by Progress Motors in 1932 in conjunction with British Amphibious Air Lines who operated a Saunders-Roe Cutty Sark Amphibian which was also named Progress. It operated from June to September and carried 348 passengers during that period.

The venture was short lived and seems to have operated only in 1932.

There is a possibility that the aircraft was owned by a member of the Armitage family or that they had an interest in it; various road operators were looking into the flying business especially in Scotland. Scottish Motor Traction operated an air taxi service and were considering scheduled services. McCrae and Dick in Inverness formed Highland Airways while John Sword, who had interests in W Alexander, had a fleet of aircraft. In England Hillman Coaches of London had formed the successful Hillman Airways.

It was not until 1935 that the Railway Air Services, whose shares were held jointly by the four main line railways, and Imperial Airways restarted a service on 15th April between Squires Gate Airport and the Isle of Man. The service was worked on behalf of the London Midland and Scottish Railway and the Isle of Man Steam Packet Company who were concerned about the development of air travel. The route was marketed under the title of "The Manx Airway" changed later to "Manx Airways".

In 1937 a new company, Isle of Man Air Services, was formed by Olley Air Services, the LMS Railway and the IOM Steam Packet who had equal shareholdings. They used aircraft transferred from the Manx Airways fleet of the Railway Air Services... Now what has all this to do with coaching? All the shares in Olley Air Services were owned by the British and Foreign Aviation whose principal shareholder was the British Electric Traction Company, at the same time a shareholder in the LMSR. The BET during the 1930s was looking at the development of air travel not so much in a competitive sense but a financial one, and had controlling interests in eight airlines by 1939. However, in October 1942 BET sold all its shares to the main line railways.

In 1946 IOM Air Services recommenced operation from Squires Gate Airport and as the years progressed different companies operated the service, sometimes as agents for British European Airways, or, as times changed, they were licensed to operate on the route in their own right. These included Lancashire Aircraft Corporation, Silver City Airways and British United Airways.

Above: In the late 1950s various services were extended across London to serve south-eastern resorts. Southdown No. **1059** (**RUF 59**), a 1956 Beadle-bodied 41-seat Leyland Tiger Cub, is seen at Mansfield after a journey from Eastbourne in June of that year. The use of a route board must have been among the last by any company in the Pool. *(JBC/GHFA)*

Below: This Yorkshire Woollen Commer, **CHD 363**, had the fleet number **778** and was bodied by Beadle as a 41-seater. It was new in 1957 and is seen at Nottingham operating from London to Dewsbury. *(JBC/GHFA)*

Ribble reopened negotiations in 1951 to arrange through bookings on their services via Squires Gate Airport not only to the Isle of Man but later to the Channel Islands, Belfast and Dublin. The through-booking arrangement was also taken up by other operators and nearly everyone who held an express service licence to Blackpool had Squires Gate added to them. As aircraft seating capacity increased so did the business and by 1962 a half-hourly service could be operating to the Isle of Man in the peak summer periods. At weekends Ribble supplied a standman, usually a senior conductor, at the airport who would keep Coliseum coach station informed of any delays or problems.

Inclusive holidays to both the Isle of Man and Channel Islands were also developed, marketed by Ribble under the "Easyway" name. These proved to be very popular from Yorkshire and in later years were called "Yorkshireway Holidays".

Consolidation of services 1961-73

In 1961 Yorkshire Traction purchased the business of Camplejohn Bros, of Darfield, which included a Blackpool service from Thurnscoe; it first appeared in the Pool timetable for the 1963 season although no "J" number was allocated.

Problems had arisen over the years with the loading arrangements at Wellington Street bus station in Leeds on summer Saturdays. Although the Traffic Commissioners had given permission for duplicate vehicles to operate from 6.30am, some two hours before the first scheduled journey, problems still arose. This was first mentioned in the 1964 summer timetable where Saville Street was shown for Saturdays then in later years Beans Ings car park, Lisbon Street and finally the railway car park opposite the bus station. It is believed this arrangement had been used prior to 1964 but not referred to in the timetable.

In the same year the layout of the winter timetable had been changed and reference to Hanson's and West Riding coordination disappeared again.

On 15th October 1967 West Yorkshire purchased the Ledgard companies and the following year saw the introduction of a Blackpool - Skipton - Yeadon - Leeds service operating Saturdays only. It was a combination of an ex-Ledgard service and the West Yorkshire Yeadon - Blackpool service and commenced from the municipal bus station in Leeds and not from Wellington Street.

In 1969 the Pool introduced a departure from Leeds at 6.30am on summer Saturdays; the thought behind this was that with traffic declining it was better to have a scheduled departure rather than have crews standing by in case passengers turned up early.

With the purchase of the West Riding Automobile Company by the National Bus Company there was an opportunity to merge some Blackpool routes. First was an application by West Riding to amend the picking up points in Blackpool to the Coliseum and Talbot Road to come into line with the Pool services. The Pool then applied for the Ossett - Blackpool service to commence from Wakefield and the corresponding licence held by West Riding would be surrendered.

In 1970 the timetable commencing in April showed West Riding as one of the operators and also indicated that the connecting facilities at Wakefield to and from Hemsworth, Pontefract and Castleford would be operated by West Riding.

Later in the year the Yorkshire (WD) involvement in the Pool had been taken over by Hebble when the coach fleet plus various licences, including the Dewsbury - Blackpool service, had been transferred to Hebble.

In 1971 application was made to operate a new service between Leeds and Blackpool via the M62/M61 motorways with West Riding as a joint operator; a further application was made for the Doncaster - Blackpool service to use the M62/M61 motorways after completion.

1972 saw the end of the Yorkshire - Blackpool Pool which was now separated into sections with Ribble and West Yorkshire holding the new licences jointly between Leeds - Blackpool/Fleetwood. A new service was licensed between Pontefract - Blackpool incorporating former West Riding picking up points to Hebble and Ribble whilst a further service was granted between Doncaster and Blackpool to Yorkshire Traction and Ribble. For the first time the ex-Wilson Haigh picking up points at New Mill and Holmfirth were

Above: Yorkshire Traction's No. **1150** (**OHE 723**) was one of six Plaxton-bodied 41-seat Leyland Tiger Cubs purchased in 1959. It is seen in Nottingham in March 1960 operating to Halifax. *(JBC/GHFA)*

Below: In 1962 Yorkshire Traction acquired three vehicles from Dan Smith & Son, of Darfield, although only one was retained. **NDA 14** was a Guy Arab underfloor-engined chassis dating from 1954, which carried a 41-seat Burlingham Seagull body. It took the number **136** in the YTC fleet. It was also in Nottingham, but heading for Bradford. *(JBC/GHFA)*

included in the timetable and received a "J" number. The services were all now marketed under the name of "Trans Pennine" in the timetable leaflets.

There were other alterations with the service from Harrogate operating Friday, Saturday, Sunday and Mondays only during the summer period and although West Yorkshire were involved it would seem W Pyne did most of the operating. At last York had been added as a picking up point with a Saturday only service via Skipton.

Nineteen-seventy-three saw further changes with Ribble and West Yorkshire renumbering their J1 - J6 routes to X81 - X86 from May 26th. The rest of the services still continued with the "J" series of route numbers. From 1st October all the services came under the control of National Travel (NBC) Ltd and all the routes were renumbered in the 200 series of the National Travel (North East) area. So ended the three coaching pools which were unique to the North: Limited Stop, Yorkshire Services and the Yorkshire - Blackpool; but there was another which continued for a further twelve years.

Yorkshire - Torbay Pool

The Torquay battle 1950-7

The last pool to originate in Yorkshire was known as the Torbay Pool. Although started only in 1967 its formation on a smaller scale could be traced back to the early 1950s.

Prior to 1951 travellers from Yorkshire could, by changing at Birmingham, travel to Cheltenham and connect at 7.00pm with a very limited number of destinations including Bristol and Weston super Mare. Passengers from Bradford, Halifax and Huddersfield could, by using the Hebble or Hanson stage carriage routes to Rochdale or Oldham, join the Yelloway direct service to Torquay or change at Cheltenham for destinations ranging across the South-West from Ilfracombe to Portsmouth. Such was the demand for the services that both Hebble and Hanson operated through coaches in the peak period from Yorkshire on hire to Yelloway and Associated Motorways.

By 1951 Yorkshire Services had been granted an early departure to Birmingham for

the summer period which, by changing, arrived in Cheltenham to connect with the 4.30pm departures, returning from Cheltenham at 2.00pm. Torquay was not available at that time due to persistent objections by the railways to extending the 4.30pm to Weston super Mare southwards.

This new facility was an immediate success with the total bookings on the connecting facility in 1952 made by Yorkshire Services amounting to £5,418 compared with £200 in 1950. As in the case of their holidays in London and Harrogate, an eight-day holiday to Bournemouth was advertised in conjunction with Hants and Dorset Motor Services. West Yorkshire provided the vehicle which stayed with the party.

In 1954 Associated Motorways, despite railway objections, finally got their grant to operate a 4.30pm to Paignton with an early timing from the resort to arrive in Cheltenham by 2.00pm. This enabled Yorkshire Services to offer via Birmingham for the first time Exeter, Torquay and Paignton from points not covered by Yelloway. Again the bookings justified the arrangement with an increase of over £3,000 in bookings on Associated Motorway connections compared with 1952. The introduction of the Torquay link helped Yorkshire Services to fight the applications made in that year by Wallace Arnold, J W Kitchin, O C Holdsworth and Hanson for summer services to Torquay. The applicants were trying to prove that the existing facilities were inadequate and passengers required through coaches and not, as at the moment, a series of linking arrangements.

Yorkshire Services did apply for a Friday evening service to Birmingham to connect with Associated Motorways to arrive in Cheltenham by 2.30am for services to Devon and Cornwall, also to increase the duplication on other Birmingham services to meet the demand. Yelloway also applied for a Huddersfield to Manchester service to replace the connecting facilities offered by Hanson. The Traffic Commissioners refused all the applications, the four independents having revised their application to a joint one instead of individually but still to no avail. There were appeals but the Minister upheld the Traffic Commissioners decisions; however, the Minister, though not against linking

Above: Chassis manufacturers usually had one or more vehicle bodied for use as demonstrators and salesmen were always anxious to place such vehicles on loan to the large company operators. The Ford Motor Company did not do outstandingly well selling into such fleets: the independent sector was a more fruitful source of orders. **EWC 971**, a Duple Trooper-bodied Ford Thames Trader 41-seater, is seen here in August 1963 running for East Yorkshire on the Scarborough to Birmingham route. East Yorkshire did not buy any Fords. *(JBC/GHFA)*

Below: Yorkshire Traction's No. **214** (**JHE 514E**), a 1967 Marshall-bodied 49-seat Leyland Leopard, is seen in August 1967 operating to Luton after one of the London routes had been cut back to terminate in that town. *(JBC/GHFA)*

arrangements as this would be against the public interest, did consider that when making applications, the operators should declare if any arrangements were to be made.

One company did succeed in obtaining a licence: Fawdon was granted an overnight service from Newcastle upon Tyne to Birmingham enabling Cheltenham to be reached for the 10.45am departures returning from there at 7.00pm. It did mean leaving Yorkshire very early, i.e. Leeds at 2.50am.

In 1956 Wallace Arnold, J W Kitchin and Hanson made another effort to gain licences to Torquay restricting them to the peak summer period. Again Yorkshire Services responded this time for two direct services, one to Torquay and the other to Bournemouth. Wallace Arnold then applied for a Bournemouth service also whilst Yelloway and Hebble applied jointly for a Bradford - Torquay service via Halifax and Huddersfield also serving Cheltenham.

In the appeal decision of the previous applications the Minister indicated that an operator was only entitled to consideration as an existing operator by reference to the services on which his vehicles ran, not by reference to services on which his vehicles worked under "on hire" arrangements to another operator.

On the first day of the hearing the worst fears of both Yorkshire Services and Yelloway were realised when the counsel for Wallace Arnold questioned the right to appear in Court of all the operators who were objecting and quoted the appeal as none of the objectors operated similar services to those applied for and therefore had no standing (locus standi) as objectors. This was upheld by the Traffic Commissioners although strongly opposed by the opposite counsel on the grounds that linking services were already recognised by the Minister. The Chairman did agree to adjourn the hearing while the objectors considered an appeal to the High Court; however Major Eastwood, the Chairman, after consultations with his staff agreed to grant locus standi to all the applicants.

When the decision was given in December only Wallace Arnold, J W Kitchin and Hanson had been granted licences, restricted to the various engineering holidays of the towns of Leeds, Bradford and Huddersfield, one town to each operator only. This led to a further round

of appeals, but the Minister upheld the Traffic Commissioners' decision. So the first round of the Yorkshire - Torbay battle had ended.

Torbay second round 1964-7

In 1964, Malcolm Barr of Wallace Arnold and Hubert Allen of Yelloway met regarding the services from Yorkshire to the South-West. Passengers still had to use Birmingham or Rochdale as the main gateways to the area. It was agreed to approach Norman Dean of Yorkshire Traction on the matter.

The following year an application appeared in the Yorkshire Traffic Area Notices & Proceedings by the Yorkshire Torbay Pool Partners of East Parade, Harrogate, the Head Office of West Yorkshire Road Car. The application consisted of a daily service between Keighley and Cheltenham with two feeders from Halifax and Leeds connecting at Wakefield with the main service. Also an additional through summer service from Keighley to Paignton again served by the two feeder services to Wakefield. There were also linking conditions to operate through vehicles across Cheltenham and Exeter on services provided by Associated Motorways or Royal Blue. It also included through bookings on various services operated by Devon General Omnibus Company. Two weeks later an amendment was published naming the partners in the Pool, these were the five companies making up the Yorkshire Services Pool, Associated Motorways, Yelloway Motor Services, Hebble Motor Services, Wallace Arnold and J W Kitchin, a total of eighteen different operators. If the licences were granted certain licences held by the last three would be surrendered.

Objections to the proposals were lodged by British Rail, Hanson, Sheffield United Tours and G C Littlewood. The last two operators had built up a range of services to the South, sometimes jointly, from Sheffield, Chesterfield and Dronfield all of which were included in the new application. Hanson still operated a seasonal service to Torquay. Two coach operators of centre holidays in the South - West also objected.

On the first day of the hearing the application fell apart with a submission from

Above: West Yorkshire Bristol RELH6G registered **LWT 369D** was fleet number **1007** and had been new in 1966 as ERG7. It had an ECW 47-seat dual-purpose body and is seen at Southgate Street, Leicester, on a short working in April 1972. *(JBC/GHFA)*

Below: Almost five years earlier, a similar chassis, but with an ECW body having 47 coach seats, was photographed in July 1967 at Newark when still very new. Fleet number **CRG2** (**PWR 858E**) was *en route* for London. *(JBC/GHFA)*

the objectors that the Pool was not a legal partnership and, this being upheld by the Chairman, the hearing was suspended.

A further application was submitted in January 1966 by the operators with individual applications for the four routes by each company with the condition that they would be operated jointly with each other and because Associated Motorways was legally treated as one operator only ten separate applications had to be made for each route required.

When the hearing was resumed the objectors again raised a point of law and applied to the High Court for an Order of Prohibition in an attempt to compel the Yorkshire Traffic Commissioners to disclose the financial particulars supplied to them by the applicants. Once again the hearing was relisted. This method of objection by using legal tactics was one used by Wallace Arnold on previous occasions over the years and they must have been surprised to have the tables turned on them.

On 9th November 1966, some 17 months after the original applications had been made, the hearing was resumed. The Traffic Commissioners granted a licence for all the four routes but not throughout the year as requested. Restrictions were imposed, especially on duplication, and the routes with through running across Cheltenham and Exeter were narrowed down to thirteen named routes. Protection was given to Sheffield United and G C Littlewood picking up points on the services which they operated. These were mainly summer weekends but had a duplication restriction on them. Block bookings whereby inclusive holidays could be offered were also prohibited. Wallace Arnold and Kitchin surrendered their Torquay licences and Hebble their special feeder service to connect at Rochdale with the Yelloway route. Yorkshire Services lost their extra duplicate allowance on the Birmingham service which had been granted to carry the connecting traffic to Cheltenham some years previously and they were also banned from advertising the Birmingham connection. It was suggested that a similar endorsement should be placed on the Yelloway licence from Rochdale but this did not happen. Fawdon Omnibus on the service from Newcastle upon Tyne had a self-imposed

restriction in their 1967 timetable showing the last picking up point on the overnight service as Harrogate to connect at Cheltenham with Associated Motorways.

The mileage agreement reached showed an interesting split with Yelloway 28.36%, Yorkshire Services 26.10%, Associated Motorways 23.52% and Wallace Arnold 22.02%.

South-West Clipper 1967-87

The time taken for the application to be heard left an uncertainty with the travelling public as to the best way to travel and for the first time television advertising was used to advertise one route, not as in the past a range of services offered by one operator. Seven 15-second slots were broadcast on the Granada Yorkshire transmitter between 22nd March and 6th April 1967 to promote the South-West Clipper as it was to be called. The first departure on 1st May from Yorkshire and operated by Yorkshire Traction carried 29 passengers and over 5,000 advance bookings had been received.

The timetable was a product of Wallace Arnold with a picture of their coach on the inside front cover. The name was taken from the Clipper ships of yesteryear: "White sails billowing against blue tropical skies, brought a new era of swiftness and sureness to travel between distant points. Timetables began to mean something at last, and so it is now" enthused the copywriter in the timetable.

By 1969 the transfer point had been moved from Wakefield to Barnsley and the Cheltenham service was operating throughout the year from 1st October.

On 1st July 1971 a through service to Bournemouth was introduced, known as the Bournemouth Clipper, and it operated on Friday evenings returning north on Saturday mornings during the summer months. In the same year, additional picking up points were added with a feeder service from York via Tadcaster, Castleford and Pontefract to Barnsley connecting with the main route.

October 1973 saw, as with the other Pools, a transfer of routes to the newly formed National Travel (NBC) Ltd. This did not mean the end of the South-West Clipper because of the involvement of Wallace Arnold, Kitchin and Yelloway. Kitchin had been a subsidiary Company of Wallace Arnold since 1959 and their mileage entitlement was included in the Wallace Arnold share. Although the services were given National Travel route numbers the timetable still continued as the "Clipper" with the Wallace Arnold design and no mention of National Express on the cover. The interchange point was changed to Sheffield from Barnsley.

By 1982 National Travel was trying to develop Bristol as an interchange point thus slowly winding down Cheltenham. This meant two daily summer services being operated: the original route between Keighley and Cheltenham, and the Halifax to Bristol bypassing Cheltenham. Interchange of passengers still took place at Sheffield between the two routes enabling a full range of picking up points and destinations to be covered. A new feeder service from Hull to Barnsley was also started. Through vehicles were operated to Paignton, Newquay, Bournemouth and Southsea on Friday evenings returning north on Saturday mornings during the summer period.

In the winter period of 1982/3 only Cheltenham was used for interchanging but again in the 1983 summer season both Cheltenham and Bristol were used. The Cheltenham coach station ceased to be an interchange point in 1984 just a few weeks before its 52nd birthday and from 22nd January all services interchanged at Bristol with the information on the timetable cover of quicker services and lower fares via Bristol but again no mention of National Express.

At the same time Yelloway Motor Services came to an agreement with National Express whereby all their long-distance services would be marketed by that company and would have National route numbers although Yelloway would still be the licence holder and operate the services.

On 27th October 1987 Yelloway withdrew completely from long-distance services to concentrate on local services within the Greater Manchester area. Meanwhile Wallace Arnold had become part of the British Coachways network which was formed in 1980 to take advantage of deregulation of long-distance services but this only lasted until 31st October 1981 when they withdrew. They still operated a London service from Leeds in opposition to National Express and this later became a joint venture marketed as a Rapide Service until Wallace Arnold withdrew from the arrangement. Their last involvement with the South-West Clipper was late in 1984 leaving the services to be operated by Yelloway and National Express until Yelloway withdrew as described above.

This really was the end of Coaching Pools in Yorkshire, but...

*...a reminder of an earlier era comes in the shape of B & B Tours Ltd **KW 7945**, a 1930 Leyland LT1 Lion with 28-seat coachwork by Burlingham. B & B, of Great Horton Road, Bradford, was taken over in 1935 by Samuel Ledgard. The vehicle was withdrawn in 1941. (JBC)*

Above: Hebble No. **446** (**JHD 830**), a Plaxton-bodied Leyland Leopard formerly in the Yorkshire Woollen District fleet, was at Westgate, Mansfield, in August 1972. In those early days of the National Bus Company, Hebble had taken over the YWD interest in the Yorkshire Services Pool, thus bringing a new fleetname on to the route. *(JBC/GHFA)*

Below: In a Leeds Road, Harrogate, view taken in September 1973, West Yorkshire's fleet number **1066** (**7937 WU**), a 1960 Bristol MW6G Eastern Coach Works 39-seater, was working on the Coventry to Newcastle Ten Cities Express. *(JBC/GHFA)*

Above: **RKH 875G**, a Marshall-bodied 49-seat Leyland Leopard dating from 1969, was fleet number **875** in the East Yorkshire fleet. It was photographed at Scarborough's Westwood coach park in September 1973 loading for London. *(JBC/GHFA)*

Below: Hall Brothers, of South Shields, was the only competitor after 1931 to the Fawdon services to Coventry. In that year, two Gilfords with Wycombe 30-seat coachwork were purchased. **CN 4398/9** are both seen in this early thirties view at Nottingham. The leading vehicle was bound for Coventry and the other for Newcastle. *(JBC/GHFA)*

Above: Hall Brothers **CU 4741**, a 1947 Duple-bodied 33-seat AEC Regal, is seen circa 1950 at Huntingdon Street bus station, Nottingham, leading three duplicates on the operator's service to Coventry. *(JBC/GHFA)*

Below: In a midsummer 1962 photograph, Hall Brothers **GCU 574**, which was a Bedford SB5 fitted with Plaxton 41-seat coachwork, and **DCU 21**, a 1960 Plaxton-bodied AEC Reliance, are seen on the way to Leicester and Coventry respectively. The Bedford was recently new and the AEC was sold at the end of that season. *(Keith Healey Collection)*

Above: Dewsbury Wakes Week in 1935 saw the usual mass exodus to various east and west coast seaside resorts. Yorkshire Woollen District's recently delivered No. **334** (**HD 5614**), a Leyland Tiger TS7 with Roe 32-seat bodywork, was loading as Duplicate No. 6 on the Blackpool service. *(JBC)*

Below: Yorkshire Traction No. **12** (**FHE 331D**), a 1966 49-seat Plaxton-bodied Leyland Leopard, is seen in about 1974 unloading passengers at Blackpool on the J7 route from Doncaster. *(Keith Healey Collection)*

Two Ribble vehicles are seen operating on the Yorkshire - Blackpool routes: No. **441 (FCK 873)** *(above)* was a 1954 Leyland Tiger Cub with attractive 44-seat service-bus bodywork produced by Saunders Roe, of Beaumaris, Anglesey. In May 1967 it was at the Coliseum coach station in Blackpool, loading passengers for a service J2 short working to Burnley. The Tiger Cub was a less-heavily engineered version of the Leyland underfloor-engined chassis, the Royal Tiger, an example of which *(below)* was Ribble's No. **925 (FCK 425)**, which dated from 1953. It is seen at Barnsley in April 1960 waiting to leave on a return timing to Blackpool on the J12 service. *(Both: JBC/GHFA)*

Upper and centre: As well as operating jointly on the Blackpool Pool in the winter months, Wallace Arnold had their own summer service to the resort. **SUG 5** *(upper)*, a 1954 AEC Reliance with Duple Elizabethan centre-entrance 41-seat coachwork, and **73 BUA**, a 1962 Reliance bodied by Plaxton, are seen parked at Blackpool waiting to take up their return timings to Yorkshire. *(Keith Healey Collection)*

Lower: The service between Harrogate and Blackpool was operated jointly by W Pyne and West Yorkshire. Pyne's 1971 Bedford SB5, bodied by Duple as a 41-seater and registered **HWU 854J**, is pictured at the Coliseum coach park in Blackpool. *(Keith Healey Collection)*

Upper: Three of W Pyne's coaches at Blackpool Coliseum. The one on the left is **XWX 912**, a 1959 Plaxton-bodied 41-seat Daimler; alongside it is **399 YG**, also a Plaxton 41-seater, but on the rather lighter Bedford SB5 chassis. *(Keith Healey Collection)*

Centre: A Hebble Motor Services Leyland-bodied Leyland Royal Tiger, No. **28** (**CCP 226**), is seen approaching Blackpool. Note the "Yorkshire Blackpool" shield on the nearside windscreen. This was to assist passengers in identifying their coach; all vehicles were supposed to show it but very few did. *(D Akrigg Collection)*

Lower: A 1938 Hebble Motor Services Duple-bodied 32-seat Leyland TS8 Tiger, No. **155** (**JX 6535**) is seen at the Coliseum parking ground. *(D Akrigg)*

Above: A 1937 Leyland TS7 Tiger, **BKW 909**, with Duple 32-seat coachwork, of B & B Tours Ltd, of Bradford, shown when brand new; at that time B & B was owned by Samuel Ledgard. B & B were joint operators with the Blackpool Pool during the winter months. *(JBC)*

Below: Hebble's mixed fleet included this 1954 Bellhouse Hartwell-bodied Leyland Royal Tiger. The "Landmaster" coachwork had 37 seats and a centre entrance. Number **36** (**ECP 500**) was photographed at the back of the Coliseum coach station in Blackpool. *(D Akrigg Collection)*

Upper: Part of the fun of travelling on the Blackpool services was never knowing what vehicle would turn up: ideal for the enthusiast; not always so for the normal passenger. Ribble No. **219** (**BDV 6**) was a 1936 Leyland TS7 Tiger, purchased from Devon General in 1949 and rebodied as a service-bus by Burlingham. The 35-seater is seen duplicating on the J1 service to Leeds. *(Keith Healey Collection)*

Centre: Not offering a great deal - if any - more comfort than the Ribble single-decker, Hebble's No. **2** (**GRR 312**), a 1946 35-seat Weymann-bodied Leyland PS1 Tiger, transferred from East Midland in 1947, is seen waiting to depart "express" to Blackpool. In both these cases, luggage would have had to be accommodated on seats. *(W J Haynes)*

Lower: This is more in line with what passengers might reasonably have expected to travel on: Yorkshire Woollen District No. **860** (**EHD 974**) was a 1960 AEC Reliance with Harrington 41-seat coachwork. It is seen in Blackpool awaiting its return timing. *(Keith Healey Collection)*

Above: This Bristol LS5G, No. **EUG66** (**TWT 119**) was one of eight delivered in 1958 to West Yorkshire as dual-purpose 41-seaters bodied by Eastern Coach Works. It was photographed operating on the J1 service between Leeds and Blackpool on which its five-cylinder engine would leave it somewhat underpowered. *(Keith Healey Collection)*

Below: A later West Yorkshire vehicle, Bristol RELH6G 47-seater **1021** (**TWX 146F**), bodied by ECW and delivered in 1968, is shown in Blackpool. The coach had been repainted into National coach livery just before the services were passed to National Travel. *(Keith Healey Collection)*

Above: The J2 service to Blackpool was home in this picture to Ribble No. **764** (**TRN 764**), a Leyland PSU3/1RT Leopard, which dated from 1964 and was fitted with a 49-seat body by Marshall, of Cambridge. The cream and crimson coach livery enhanced the rather bland body styling. *(Keith Healey Collection)*

Below: In another coach park scene at the resort, Hebble's No. **178** (**GCP 7**) has completed its journey to Blackpool. An AEC Reliance dating from 1956, the 44-seat service-bus bodywork was by Willowbrook. *(Keith Healey Collection)*

Above: Another Ribble/Hebble contrast starts with Ribble's No. **266** (**DRN 130**) on the J1 Blackpool to Leeds run. A 1951 Leyland HR44 Olympic, it had 44 seats in its Weymann service-bus bodywork. *(Keith Healey Collection)*

Below: Stage-carriage comfort standards again for passengers to Blackpool on Hebble's **KCP 890**, which was No. **188** in the fleet. This was another Willowbrook-bodied AEC Reliance, this time a 1959 43-seater. *(Keith Healey Collection)*

Above: Hanson, of Huddersfield, like Wallace Arnold, operated jointly with the Pool in the winter months to Blackpool. Hanson had their own service from Huddersfield to the resort in the summer. This AEC Reliance, No. **346** (**KVH 344**), is seen parked between journeys. *(Keith Healey Collection)*

Below: In 1952 Yorkshire Services were operating through coaches to Cheltenham on hire to Associated Motorways from Birmingham. Yorkshire Traction No. **676** (**HE 9530**), a 1940 Leyland TS8 Tiger, was carrying its third body, a 1932 Burlingham 31-seat unit fitted to it in 1952. The vehicle was at Nottingham, returning to Leeds, with its destination sticker and on hire label visible in the nearside front window. *(JBC/GHFA)*

Above: East Yorkshire No. **923** (**BKH 923K**), a Plaxton-bodied 49-seat Leyland Leopard PSU3B/4R, was in a blue and white version of the NBC's "local coach" livery when photographed in Mansfield Road, Nottingham, operating between Hull and Cheltenham on the South-West Clipper. *(JBC/GHFA)*

Below: Hebble No. **71** (**RJX 871**), a 1963 Leyland PSU3/3R Leopard, again with Plaxton coachwork, but to an earlier design seating 47, is seen *en route* for Torquay. In its windscreen is a sticker advertising Paignton as a further destination, as well as the South-West Clipper emblem. *(D Akrigg Collection/M Fenton)*

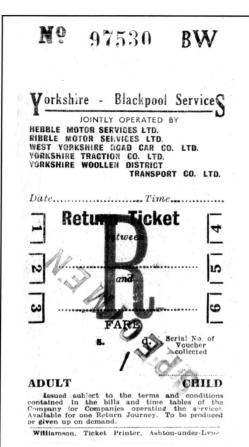

1A

Nº 97530 BW

Yorkshire - Blackpool Services

JOINTLY OPERATED BY

HEBBLE MOTOR SERVICES LTD.
RIBBLE MOTOR SERVICES LTD.
WEST YORKSHIRE ROAD CAR CO. LTD.
YORKSHIRE TRACTION CO. LTD.
YORKSHIRE WOOLLEN DISTRICT
TRANSPORT CO. LTD.

Date.................... Time...........

Return Ticket

Between

and

FARE

s.   d.

Serial No. of
Voucher
collected

ADULT   **CHILD**

Issued subject to the terms and conditions
contained in the bills and time tables of the
Company (or Companies operating the service).
Available for one Return Journey. To be produced
or given up on demand.

Williamson, Ticket Printer. Ashton-under-Lyne

1

Nº 25034 A

YORKSHIRE SERVICES

Jointly Operated by

West Yorkshire Road Car Co. Ltd.
Yorkshire Woollen District
Transport Co. Ltd.
Yorkshire Traction Co. Ltd.
East Yorkshire Motor Services Ltd.
East Midland Motor Services Ltd.

DATE ....   TIME ....

Single Ticket
FROM

TO

FARE

No. of Seat   s.   d.   SERIAL No.
Reservation   OF VOUCHER
                             COLLECTED

ADULT   **CHILD**

Issued subject to the terms and conditions contained in the bills and time tables of the Company
(or Companies operating the service). Available
for one Single Journey. To be produced or
given up on demand.

Williamson, Ticket Printer, Ashton-under-Lyne

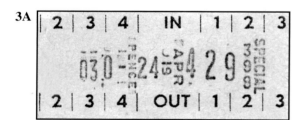

3A

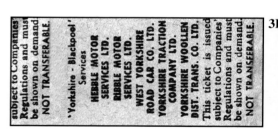

3

4A

Yorkshire - Blackpool Services

From	Voucher No.
To	Class
S FARE D	Date

W 00048   Bell Punch Company, Limited, London.

SEE CONDITIONS ON BACK

4

YORKSHIRE SERVICES

From	Voucher No.
To	Class
S FARE D	Date

W 00139   Bell Punch Company, Limited, London.

SEE CONDITIONS ON BACK

```
Operated Jointly by          YORKSHIRE   YORKSHIRE TRACTION
                                                  Co.  Ltd
WEST YORKSHIRE                               EAST YORKSHIRE
  ROAD CAR CO. LTD.                          MOTOR  SERVICES LTD.
YORKSHIRE                                    EAST MIDLAND
  WOOLLEN DISTRICT TRANSPORT CO. LTD.  SERVICES  MOTOR SERVICES LTD.
```

SINGLE) Delete word
RETURN) not required

№   3004   C

Between ....)
and ....)   via ....

Outward date ....Time ....   **F**

Pick up at **1**

Return date .... Time **2**

Pick up at ....

Seat Reservation   Number of {..........Adults @.................each
No. ....   Passengers {........Children @.................each

TOTAL FARE PAID £   :   :

Issued by .... Date .... Agency No. ....

No(s). of Tickets issued by Cond. in lieu...................

This Voucher will be withdrawn by the Conductor and Tickets issued in lieu
thereof. Issued subject to the terms and conditions contained in the bills and
time tables of the operating companies.   Williamson, Printer, Ashton

Tickets: In 1939 conductors on Yorkshire Services and Yorkshire - Blackpool routes used the written book tickets *(examples 1A and 1B)* for passengers paying on the vehicle. Advance-booked passengers would have a voucher *(example 2)*, which would be exchanged for a written book ticket by the conductor. The amount of casual traffic at that time was 5% on Yorkshire Services, which showed the need for advance booking because of duplication restriction, against 22% on the Blackpool routes who had paid on the vehicle.

With the recommencement in 1946/7, the Yorkshire-Blackpool services continued with written book tickets but by 1965, with the introduction of the Universal vouchers some years previously, the system had changed and there was little consistency with only Hebble using book tickets; Ribble and West Yorkshire had now resorted to the Setright system with a special green ticket roll detailing on the back the names of the five operators *(examples 3A and 3B)*. Yorkshire Traction and Yorkshire Woollen issued Universal vouchers for casual bookings. Yorkshire Services continued with the written book ticket before transferring to Universal vouchers. It would seem that, for a short time, the Bellgraphic system was also used *(examples 4A and 4B)* on both pools. This would account for the emergency type of ticket printed by Bell Punch in the same format but in strips of four and the ticket was card instead of paper. This was used by Hebble in the sixties. In 1973 the green Setright ticket was withdrawn by Ribble and West Yorkshire after the split in the Pools operation and was replaced by the normal white Setright roll used by each company. *(All tickets illustrated by courtesy of the West Yorkshire Information Service)*

This timetable issued in 1930 under the heading Yorkshire Services shows the start of the jointly operated services to London. (*Keith Healey Collection*)

EXPRESS
AND
LIMITED STOP
SERVICES
BETWEEN
YORKSHIRE
AND
BLACKPOOL

(also FLEETWOOD)

Including

LEEDS, BRADFORD, KEIGHLEY, BARNSLEY, WAKEFIELD, DEWSBURY, HUDDERSFIELD, HALIFAX, &c.

Jointly Operated by
Ribble Motor Services, Ltd.
West Yorkshire Road Car Co., Ltd.
Yorkshire (W.D.) Electric Tramways, Ltd.
Yorkshire Traction Co., Ltd.
Hebble Motor Services, Ltd.
W. Armitage & Sons, Ltd.
Walker Taylor & Sons, Ltd.
Wood Bros. (Blackpool), Ltd.

TIME TABLE & FARES LISTS
FEBRUARY 1st to APRIL 12th, 1935 (incl.)

For List of Enquiry Offices and Agents see pages 11 and 12.

So far as licensing regulations permit **RETURN TICKETS ARE INTER-AVAILABLE ON ANY OF THE BUSES OPERATING THE JOINT SERVICES** and also on a number of other services independently operated by certain of the Companies concerned.

TRAVEL BY ROAD

After the refusal of the North Western and Yorkshire Traffic Commissioners to grant joint licences, a special timetable was issued on 1st February 1935, showing the services of all the eight operators and introducing the "J" route numbers. *(Keith Healey Collection)*

In 1935, after the last competitor had been purchased, this timetable was issued incorporating Yorkshire Services, East Midland, and the London - Midlands - Yorkshire operation, as well as Phillipson's route to Scarborough. *(Courtesy West Yorkshire Information Service)*

In 1947 Hall Brothers issued a full-colour brochure for their service on the Newcastle upon Tyne to Coventry route. *(Keith Healey Collection)*

DAILY
EXPRESS COACH SERVICE

LONDON
MIDLANDS
YORKSHIRE

operated by

COMMENCING		
JULY 18th, 1947	- -	from YORKSHIRE
JULY 19th, 1947	- -	to YORKSHIRE

Above: Also in 1947, upon the recommencement of the London service, an attractive leaflet was printed by West Yorkshire on behalf of the Yorkshire Services Pool. *(Keith Healey Collection)*

Right: The Fawdon Bus Company route was included with the Yorkshire Services timings in this 1947 timetable. *(Keith Healey Collection)*

COVENTRY
BIRMINGHAM
YORKSHIRE
NEWCASTLE

DAILY

Luxury Coach Services

by

YORKSHIRE SERVICES

AND

FAWDON BUS COMPANY

TIME TABLE and
FARES LISTS

Ref No. 2658

Daily Coach Services to . . .
YORKSHIRE

TIME TABLES and FARE LISTS

23rd October, 1951 to 28th May, 1952

For details of increased services during the Easter Holidays,
10th to 16th April, 1952, see later announcements.

YORKSHIRE
JOINT SERVICES
BLACKPOOL

You see more by road

Above: Printed with a yellow background, the 1951 winter timetable for the Yorkshire - Blackpool services shows the special Pool emblem and a coach approaching the industrial heart of Yorkshire from Blackpool. *(Keith Healey Collection)*

Right: By 1962, the Fawdon Bus Company had been wound up and replaced by the Ten Cities Express. This timetable cover shows the connections available via Birmingham to the South West using the facilities of Associated Motorways. *(Courtesy West Yorkshire Information Service)*

NEWCASTLE TO COVENTRY

10 CITIES EXPRESS

Summer Time Table - Daily from 7th June to 17th September, 1962

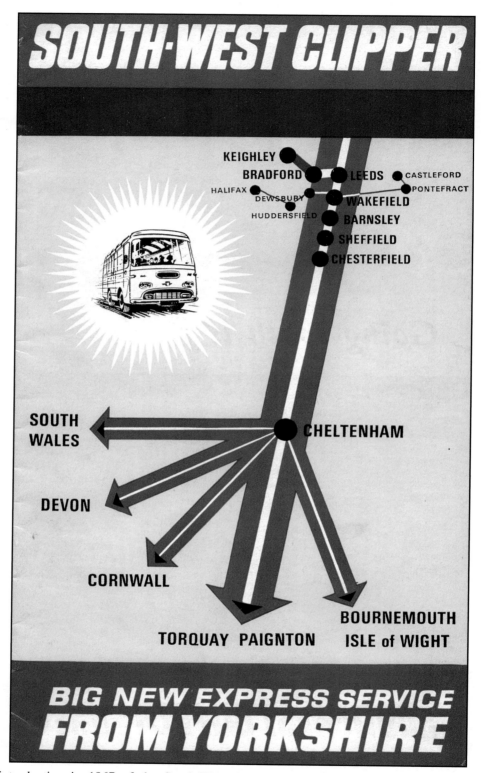

The introduction in 1967 of the South-West Clipper from Yorkshire to Cheltenham onwards produced this colourful timetable from Wallace Arnold on the Pool's behalf. The name was retained through to the late 1980s. *(Keith Healey Collection)*